Stop Nursing Home Abuse in Ohio

What to Look For
What to Do
(Second Edition)

Slater & Zurz LLP
Attorneys at Law
Akron • Canton • Cleveland • Columbus

Stop Nursing Home Abuse in Ohio
What to Look For
What to Do

By: Slater & Zurz LLP
Attorneys at Law

©Copyright 2015 by Slater & Zurz LLP
All Rights Reserved. This book or any portion thereof may not be reproduced or used in any manner whatsoever without the express written permission of Slater & Zurz LLP.

Printed in the United States of America

Second Printing 2015

For permission to reproduce or to order additional copies of this book, contact Slater & Zurz LLP by calling 1-800-297-9191 or send a written request to:

Slater & Zurz LLP
One Cascade Plaza, Suite 2210
Akron, Ohio 44308

TABLE OF CONTENTS

Introduction   1

Chapter 1:
Nursing Home Abuse Statistics   4

Chapter 2:
Checklist to Avoid Nursing Home Abuse and Neglect   9

Chapter 3:
Nursing Home Negligence Defined by Ohio Law   25

Chapter 4:
Rights of Nursing Home Residents   27

Chapter 5:
Confirming Suspicions of Abuse or Neglect   30

Chapter 6:
Selecting the Right Nursing Home for Alzheimer's Patients   32

Chapter 7:
Elder Abuse vs. Nursing Home Abuse   36

Chapter 8:
Legal Actions That Can Be Taken Against Nursing Homes   38

Chapter 9:
Understaffed Nursing Homes — 41

Chapter 10:
Misuse and Overuse of Drugs and Medications — 49

Chapter 11:
Falls in Nursing Homes — 52

Chapter 12:
Broken Bones and Fractures — 57

Chapter 13:
Malnutrition and Dehydration — 60

Chapter 14:
Feeding Tubes — 66

Chapter 15:
Bedsores — 70

Chapter 16:
Seven Entrapment Zones of Bedrails — 72

Chapter 17:
Misuse of Restraints — 74

Chapter 18:
Clostridium Difficile Infection — 76

Chapter 19:
Physical Therapy Abuse or Neglect   78

Chapter 20:
Inaccurate and Altered Medical Charts   82

Chapter 21:
Financial Abuse   84

Chapter 22:
Wandering Away from a Nursing Home   88

Chapter 23:
Food Quality   92

Chapter 24:
Injuries While Being Moved
Within a Nursing Home   96

Chapter 25:
Injuries While Being Transported
Outside a Nursing Home   98

Chapter 26:
Necessity of an Autopsy in a
Nursing Home Abuse Death Claim   100

Chapter 27:
Examples of Nursing Home Abuse   103

Chapter 28:
Why You Should Talk to a Nursing Home Abuse Attorney and How an Attorney Can Help with No Out of Pocket Costs to You   110

The Authors   115

Introduction

The care and supervision of loved ones are entrusted with nursing homes, assisted living and managed care facilities throughout Ohio. While most provide excellent care, supervision and quality of life, some nursing homes are not worthy of that trust. It's a harsh reality that a loved one may become a victim of unexplained injuries, verbal and/or physical abuses, substandard care, neglect or unexpected death.

Nursing homes and managed care facilities are highly regulated operations. There are specific rules and requirements in place to protect residents and patients. These facilities must satisfy those requirements.

Errors in administering medication, dehydration, malnutrition, falls, broken bones, fractures and other injuries may occur if staff members do not receive the proper certifications and training.

Poor hiring practices may result in some facilities retaining staff members with a history of neglect, abuse and carelessness. Sexual assaults by other residents or employees of the care facility are unthinkable acts, however, they do happen.

These are just a few examples of what can occur in Ohio nursing homes and long term care facilities. Your loved one deserves the respect and dignity that comes with proper care. A level of service that falls short of that requires your action.

No one knows your loved one better than you. You may notice the signs and your gut feeling, intuition or suspicions may tell you something is wrong. If questions or concerns have begun to form in your mind, you owe it to yourself and your loved one to get help and answers.

This book is intended to provide you with a general understanding of nursing home abuse and neglect. It provides an outline of things to look for in order to avoid nursing home abuse, and warning signs that abuse or neglect may be occurring. It also provides you with guidance on where to turn for help and actions you can take to stop nursing home abuse and prevent it from happening to someone else.

Slater & Zurz LLP
Call us for a free consultation with an attorney experienced with handling nursing home abuse cases throughout Ohio:
1-800-297-9191

DISCLAIMER

The information contained within this book is for informational use only. This book is not intended to be used as legal advice nor should it be used as legal advice. Furthermore, no attorney-client relationship has been created or formed as a result of receiving, purchasing or reading this book.

Cases involving nursing home abuse and neglect are unique, complex and involve many different legal issues where the outcome of the case is dependent on the particulars of that specific case.

You should consult with a qualified attorney who is licensed and who has experience with nursing home abuse and neglect cases in the state of Ohio.

If you would like a free consultation with Mr. Martin Delahunty, our lead nursing home abuse attorney at the Ohio law firm of Slater & Zurz LLP, please call 1-800-297-9191 or visit stopohionursinghomeabuse.com and send a message from the website.

Chapter 1
Nursing Home Abuse Statistics

Although nursing homes are involved in a variety of lawsuits for different kinds of abuse and negligence, and although the publicity surrounding Ohio nursing home abuse and negligence seems endless, there are still a shocking number of nursing homes that fail to provide their residents with the standard of care that they deserve.

Here is a compilation of real, but shocking, recent statistics that shine a light on just how little so many of these facilities care about our loved ones.

- In 2007, there were 257,872 complaints against nursing homes relating to quality of care, facilities, staffing, and other factors. This averages out to twenty complaints per nursing home in this country.

- In 2005, 91.7% of America's nursing homes were cited by health inspectors for at least one deficiency.

- More than 30% of all nursing homes have had some form of resident abuse, whether it's by staff or other residents. These include malnutrition, physical abuse, psychological distress, exploitation, neglect, and sexual abuse.

- Much of the time, those who abuse nursing home residents are not strangers: 90% of them are known to the victim. That includes staff members, other residents, or familiar visitors.

- A study of death certificates for the year 1999 indicated that as many as 5000 nursing home deaths were caused by negligence, including starvation, dehydration, or bedsores as the cause of death. Two years later, in 2001, one out of four nursing homes was cited for death or serious injury to a resident.

- Patients are being overmedicated. Two studies indicate that a high percentage of nursing home patients are receiving anti-psychotic drugs. One study found a third of patients were on these medications, and another study found that more than 90% of nursing home patients were on anti-psychotics.

- A primary cause of harm to nursing home patients is an inadequate, untrained, or even criminal staff. There are no national requirements for criminal background checks for nursing home workers, and one estimate says that there is at least one person with a criminal background employed in every single nursing home.

- Understaffing is another major problem. Many nursing homes do not have the staff levels necessary to properly care for their patients. Often, the ratio of nurses' aides to patients is 1:15, but it can go as high as 30. The recommendation is 1:3 during a meal and 1:6 during non-meal times.

That makes policing residents very difficult, even if abuse is out in the open. In one investigation, 12 nurses observed aggression between residents 30 times in an 8-hour shift. And many nursing home patients have no one else to look out for them: more than 50% of nursing home residents don't have close relatives. Many residents of nursing homes are without family support that can watch out for neglect or abuse. In fact, it is estimated that only about 20% of nursing home abuse cases are ever reported. Many nursing home residents do not have the mental presence or confidence to report abuse for them, and it may go unnoticed by family and other caretakers, or it may be covered up by the staff.

As the U.S. population ages, baby boomers are looking at a shortfall of nursing home beds. In 2008, there were only 1.8 million total nursing facility beds, but there were 18.8 million people aged 65-74, and 14.7 million people aged 75 or older.

As the cost of nursing homes will only continue to rise. The annual average cost for a room at a private nursing home in 2003 was $66,000; the average annual cost for a private nursing home room may be $175,000 by 2021.

It is impossible to know how common Ohio nursing home abuse is because it is so underreported. Some national statistics may help us understand the scope of the problem.

According to the National Research Council, between 1 million and 2 million people over the age of 65 have been injured or exploited by a person who is supposed to be providing them care or protection. This statistic relates to elders in general, not those in nursing homes specifically, but there is reason to believe that number is also high.

A federal study conducted in 2001 found that 31% of nursing homes received citations for abusing their residents. A third of these violations caused actual harm to residents or put them in immediate danger of injury or death.

Unfortunately, these numbers are unlikely to decrease any time soon. In fact, the situation may get a whole lot worse. More than one million Americans currently live in nursing homes or assisted living communities, but this number will certainly grow as Baby Boomers reach retirement age.

The best way to combat nursing home abuse is to make sure that all offenses are appropriately punished. This is hard, however, because residents are afraid to report abuse for a variety of reasons. Sometimes they are explicitly threatened by the abuser and fear that their abuse will get worse if they tell anyone. Other times, they worry that people won't believe them or will think they're developing dementia.

Sometimes, lines of communication with family members have already been damaged due to disagreements over whether the resident actually belongs in an elder care facility. This makes it especially hard to reach out to family members when abuse starts.

Then there are those residents who simply don't have any family or friends to tell. If their complaints to nursing home staff are not acted upon, they don't know where else to turn for help. In all, it is estimated that only one in 14 instances of elder abuse are reported to the appropriate authorities. The number is even lower for financial abuse specifically.

Nursing homes may not explicitly condone abuse, but they frequently fail to uphold their duty to prevent it.

Chapter 2
Checklist to Avoid Nursing Home Abuse and Neglect

Seeking nursing home care for a loved one is possibly one of the most anguishing decisions a family will make. Family members can be overwrought with mixed emotions ranging from guilt, because they are no longer able to care for their cherished one, to anxiety concerning the quality of care that their loved one will receive in the nursing home. The tremendous amount of pressure felt by family members to find a reliable nursing home can be very stressful.

You may have time to research nursing homes or you may be under some deadline to find one immediately. In any case, it's good to have a plan of action.

Nursing homes offer two levels of service and they are as follows:

Skilled Nursing Facilities: These offer continual nursing service on a 24-hour basis to residents requiring extensive care or rehabilitative care by registered nurses, based on treatment or instructions prescribed by the resident's physician.

Intermediate Care Facilities: Best suited for residents with chronic health conditions but who do not require intensive care. The staff in these facilities usually consists of licensed practical nurses and nurses' aides who provide medical, social, and rehabilitative services.

Nursing homes must be licensed by the state in which they operate. In addition, nursing homes must be certified by the federal government before they can receive Medicaid or Medicare payments. This is crucial.

Try to select at least three homes to visit. The selection should be based on the following:

The patient's specific health issues: For instance, someone recovering from hip or knee replacement surgery, or recovering from a condition such as a stroke, should seek the hospital-like setting offered by the Skilled Nursing Care facilities. A family member with Alzheimer's disease or Dementia would benefit from an Intermediate Care facility which has staff and physical space devoted to the care of those patients.

Location, location, location: Choose facilities that will be easily accessible for visits from family and friends.

Your loved one's spiritual and cultural needs and preferences: Make sure the facility will accommodate the practices of your cherished one's spiritual or religious affiliation and/or cultural background.

Payment Methods Accepted: If the family member has private insurance, only certain facilities may be covered. Not all facilities accept Medicaid patients or those whose financial resources may run dry in the near future. Be vigilant and inform yourself in advance about the possibility of your cherished one being faced with an abrupt move if his or her funds are exhausted.

Tours and Inspections: Once you have filtered out the homes that do not fit your loved one's requirements you can now focus on the ones that have aroused your interest. Call each facility and arrange a visit with the administrator or admissions director. It is recommendable to visit the nursing home in the late morning or early afternoon to observe the noon meal. This will give you the opportunity to take note of the interaction between residents and the general ambience and personality of the home. Attempt to visit a second time during the weekend or evening because these are generally times when nursing homes reduce their staff and services.

Questions to Ask: Make a list of questions tailored to your family member's particular needs and circumstances prior to your first visit. The following questions are typical examples of what you may ask the administrator:

> **How many other residents have similar medical needs as my family member?**

Do at least some staff members have specific training to care for residents with a similar diagnosis?

If there is a conflict with a roommate, what accommodations can be made?

Ask questions regarding food served, spiritual needs, available activities, and any other question you may think is pertinent to your loved one's needs and comfort. Ask the same questions of all the homes visited so you can make a comparison. Making a summary of all the replies while still there can help you remember what each home offered.

Finally, every certified nursing home undergoes annual state and federal inspection surveys. You can ask the nursing home administrator to show you the results of the home's most recent government inspection survey and have him or her explain the results.

What to Look for During a Tour:

Certification. Make sure the facility and its administrators are licensed by the state and that the home is certified for Medicare and Medicaid. Review the state health department's report and contact the Nursing Home state investigator to see if there have been any serious problems at the home.

Staff. The licensed staff of nursing homes can range from certified nursing assistants to registered nurses, while some homes also employ nurse practitioners. In appraising the facility's staff, take note of the following:

- **Is the staff-to-patient ratio adequate?**

- **Is the staff friendly and attentive?**

- **Do they show a respectful attitude towards the patients?**

- **Are they clean, well-groomed and work well as a team in an organized manner?**

Residents: Observe whether the residents look well-groomed and appropriately dressed. Check to see if the residents are engaged in various activities and whether they are able to go outdoors. Do the residents seem content and reasonably alert? Is the staff stimulating them in some way?

Living Quarters: Are the rooms clean, tidy, and odor-free? The rooms should also have at least one window and adequate privacy. Take note as to whether residents can decorate their rooms to some degree with their personal belongings.

Safety: Look for smoke detectors, call buttons, handrails in the hallways, grab bars in the bathrooms, and other accessories aimed at preventing accidents.

Final Choice: Once you have chosen the homes based on location, quality of care, and ability to care for the particular needs of your family member, the final determinant will be your intuition.

Reading the Admissions Agreement: When visiting each facility, ask the administrator for a written statement of the basic monthly charges and what services are covered, including the level of nursing care, therapy, room size, number of meals and housekeeping services. Beware of institutions that require the payment of a large deposit that may "lock in" a patient who depletes his or her life savings to make this payment. This may make it impossible for the resident to move elsewhere for lack of funds. If a deposit is mandatory, investigate the possibility of making monthly installments into a deposit fund. Also, be aware that a nursing home cannot require a pre-payment or admissions deposit from a patient relying on Medicare or Medicaid for payment of its services and care.

Some non-profit facilities require that a patient sign over all their assets to become the institution's property after their death. However, it is illegal for a for-profit institution to follow this same procedure. Make sure you understand these stipulations before signing an agreement.

Paying for Long-Term Care: Long-term care can be very expensive. It is of utmost concern to most families as to how they are going to tackle the costs of this type of service and care. A few of the financial strategies used today are as follows:

Reverse Mortgages are loans that allow seniors to tap the equity in their home. The bank agrees to lend the senior a percentage of the home's market value that does not have to be repaid until the homeowner's death and the house is sold.

Life Insurance policies are another possible alternative. The owner of a life insurance policy can borrow against its cash value, therefore using the policy as collateral for a loan. The loan plus interest is then deducted from the death benefit when the insured dies. Also, seniors who are struggling to pay premiums on life insurance policies have the option of selling their policies to provide funds for their long term care. Consult an accountant, lawyer, or other financial expert before signing this kind of agreement.

Viatical Settlements are agreements in which a company pays a terminally ill person a percentage of the face value of the individual's life insurance in cash before their death. As a result, the company then becomes the new beneficiary of the policy. Again, consult an accountant, lawyer, or other financial professional before signing this type of agreement.

How to Evaluate

The Ohio Department of Health offers valuable information on their website as follows:

www.odh.ohio.gov will assist consumers in evaluating a nursing home or in comparing various nursing homes. The website offers vital information for consumers on how to choose a nursing home and provides links to a network of inspection results for all nursing homes in Ohio.

Nursing homes are inspected by the State every 9 to 15 months to assess compliance with federal standards of care such as adequate staffing, quality of care, and cleanliness of facilities. More detailed information about individual nursing homes in Ohio is available at the federal government website, **www.medicare.gov**. This site contains a search tool to locate information on every Medicare and Medicaid certified nursing home and hospital in the country. At this website you can obtain information about any nursing home you are thinking of such as information on the nursing home amenities, the composition of the resident population and the results of the home's most recent state inspection. You can also request a comparison of two or more nursing homes.

Where to Get Help – Complaints

The complaint hot line is 1-800-342-0553 for anyone suspecting elder abuse and/or abuse of your loved one. Do not be afraid to use this hotline as it is there for your family member's protection. Please be aware that signs of neglect are also found under the umbrella of what is considered abuse.

Ohio inspectors use the Long Term Care Survey Manual in their investigations, as it details federal regulations and provides a thorough analysis of care required. Examination of a complaint is completed by surveyors after receiving relevant documents from the Ohio Dept of Health.

The Ohio Dept of Health Complaint Unit is located in Columbus, OH. The address is as follows:

Ohio Department of Health
Nursing Homes / Facilities
246 North High St- 3rd floor
P.O. Box 118
Columbus, OH 43215
Tel: 614-752-9524 / Fax: 614-564-2450

Lists of enforcement actions may be obtained by contacting the Bureau of Regulatory Compliance at 614-644-6220.

Inspection reports for individual homes or residential care are available from the Bureau of Information & Operation Support at 614-644-7238. The cost of receiving these is minimal.

The Centers for Medicare and Medicaid Services (CMS) gave one in five Medicare/Medicaid-certified nursing homes the lowest rating (one star, out of a possible five), based on quality of care, staffing, and health inspections.

Judged against more than 180 Medicaid-directed regulatory standards, each one-star home had an average of 14 quality-of-life or safety deficiencies in a one-or two-year period. In November 2009, University of California researchers released a report showing that nationwide, violations of nursing home regulations rose 8% from 2003 to 2008, with some states showing increases as high as 71%.

A Government Accountability Office report released in August 2009 found that for-profit homes showed the worst performance.

There are a lot of things to consider when evaluating a nursing home for yourself or a family member.

Coverage Considerations

You need to be up to speed on Medicare and Medicaid coverage - and how the two differ. For eligible patients - people 65 or older, some disabled people under 65, and people of all ages with end-stage renal disease – Medicare covers up to 100 days of necessary skilled nursing care following a three-day minimum hospital stay.

The first 20 Medicare days are paid in full; after that, the resident pays daily copay, which may be covered by a client's Medigap insurance policy, if he or she has one. Nursing home residents whose room and board are not covered by Medicare may still look to Medicare for health coverage for hospital stays, medical care, and medications.

Medicaid is a health care safety net funded by federal and state governments for people who meet resource-eligibility requirements. It pays for nursing home care as long as the resident remains income-eligible and has long-term care needs. Medicaid clients pay a monthly deductible set by state law, and covered services vary from state to state.

Nationwide, more than two-thirds of nursing home residents receive help from Medicaid. So when offering advice on nursing home choices, you should be aware of relevant state Medicaid eligibility rules, including asset exhaustion requirements, income retention, and spousal impoverishment rights. You should also be familiar with state-based variations in Medicaid-covered services and be able to point your client to state agencies, advocacy organizations, or ombudsman services that handle Medicaid questions and concern in your state.

Even if your resources are ample, it's wise to consider a facility's Medicaid certification at the start. For one thing, Medicaid-certified facilities are evaluated annually and must meet federal and state certification, licensing, and performance standards. Moreover, statistics show that most long-term nursing home residents will deplete their resources enough to meet Medicaid eligible standards at some time during their stay, and federal law prohibits Medicaid-certified homes from evicting residents or terminating necessary services when residents become Medicaid eligible.

On the other hand, the ability to pay privately for coverage – or coverage under Medicare's 100-day post-hospital skilled-nursing-care benefit – may help you gain admission to the nursing home of your choice, as private payments and Medicare reimbursement rates easily exceed Medicaid reimbursement rates.

Whether you pay privately or with public support, know what services will be covered in a nursing facility's rate structure. Private-pay residents, in particular, should ascertain which services are included in the facility's basic daily rate and which services, such as therapy, medications, lab tests and physician services, are billed separately.

You should also ask about rate-increase history, policies, and notification requirements. You should understand your rights under state and federal law when it comes to the facility's proposed financial and legal terms, such as paying a security deposit, placing funds in trust with the facility, guaranteeing financial responsibility, giving donations in return for guaranteed bed space, or receiving notice of and assistance with Medicaid eligibility.

Admissions paperwork that includes an agreement to arbitrate grievances should be handled with extreme caution. These arbitration clauses limit your ability to get recourse for violations of care and fiduciary violations.

Some states have attempted to standardize nursing home admissions agreements to prevent such abuses. Even so, it is always wise to have an attorney review the financial terms of any admissions agreement before signing it.

Information about the nursing home's administrative structure and its stability may also be important to your choice. From Medicare's Nursing Home Compare program, you can quickly learn whether a home is a for-profit chain, or a not-for-profit operation, which often correlates with a home's staffing levels and, as noted above, with quality of care. You can check on the home's staffing levels, stability of the current administration, and turnover. These also tend to correlate with quality of care and amenability to suit and summons if things go wrong and litigation ensues.

You may be interested in the activities, governance rights, and advocacy roles of resident or family councils. Ask about the ease of family visitation, which is an easy way to keep tabs on treatment and care. Look closely at compliance with administrative regulations regarding licensing and accreditation, required postings, notices, needs-assessment and care planning, safety inspections, and money management as indicators of administrators' concern for the residents' rights and needs.

Assessing Quality of Care

Quality of care is certainly one of the chief criteria for selecting a nursing home.

You should scrutinize inspection reports, medical records, and staff logs for indicators of deficiencies in staffing, training, supervision, policy development, equipment, assessment, planning and oversight. But that's mostly after-the-fact investigation; looking for these red flags before you sign an admissions agreement is a different matter. Here are some simple suggestions to make the process more manageable.

> **Consider special needs**. If the person has special medical needs - for instance, respiratory therapy or a specialized dementia unit - make sure that prospective homes offer those services and have a history of compliance with the necessary certification standards. Also, make sure that certified facilities do not regularly reject appropriate patients simply for staffing convenience or cost control.
>
> **Check the records**. Look carefully at the facility's record on key quality measures: infection control, pressure sores, weight loss, bladder control, use of restraints, mobility and daily living skills, depression, anxiety and pain treatment. As CMS cautions, these measures are not standards of care, but they do offer a snapshot of each home in comparison to others. And they often point to

problems that may show up in resident complaints, CMS investigations, and even litigation.

Visit the facility. When you do, take along one of the many checklists available from federal, state and advocacy sources. Pay particular attention to details about hiring practices; accommodation of personal needs; thoroughness of assessments and care plans, and regularity of reviews; care with continence, hydration, and nutrition; use of feeding tubes, sedation, and restraints; medication protocols; pressure ulcers and personal care; environment and activities; emergency procedures; and billing and administration.

Look for "culture change" programs and practices. "Culture change" is a term used by nursing home researchers and advocates describing actions taken to improve quality of care and quality of life by "de-institutionalizing services and individualizing care." It grew out of the 1987 Federal Nursing Home Reform Act, which mandates that each nursing home "care for its residents in such a manner and in such an environment as will promote maintenance or enhancement of the quality of life of each resident." Homes that emphasize this protocol use "person-directed practices" that allow residents to make daily life choices on their own, emphasize the continuity of relationships between residents and staff, and make the care environment as homelike, intergenerational, and intimate as possible.

A CMS study offers a checklist, titled *Artifacts of Culture Change* that measures a facility against culture-change criteria. This guide can be of great help in identifying quality of care and quality of life factors that are important in any nursing home setting.

Chapter 3
Nursing Home Negligence Defined by Ohio Law

Ohio law provides that nursing home residents have a right to complain about any neglect or abuse that they experience while in a nursing home. Under common law, the standard of care in nursing homes is what a reasonably careful person would do under the same or similar circumstances.

The Ohio Nursing Home Bill of Rights provides additional protections that, in certain cases, go above and beyond what the common law might allow.

A nursing home (or its owner) can be held liable for negligence if the injured party can show that:

- The nursing home's owner or its employees breached a duty of care that was owed to the injured person;

- The person's injury was actually caused by such breach;

- The conduct of nursing home owner or his or her employee was what caused the injury.

In order to prove this, a person who decides to sue a nursing home may want to consider offering expert medical testimony about what are or are not proper practices in the industry, as well as the treatments or procedures that are typically used in a given situation. If the lack of care or skill by the nursing home is so obvious that the average person would realize it based on his or her own common knowledge and experience, medical testimony may not be necessary.

Ordinarily, nursing homes enter into contracts with their residents that set forth the services that the nursing homes will provide, as well as the price for those services. If the alleged abuse or neglect of the nursing home or its employees is in contradiction with the promises made in the contract regarding the care of residents, the nursing home can be sued under a breach of contract theory. Some contracts require only that the home give such services as are "reasonably necessary" for their resident's well-being; however, even under this standard, the nursing home could be found negligent if it failed to fulfill the basic needs of the resident.

Chapter 4
Rights of Nursing Home Residents

A few years ago, hospitals started to post lists of "Patients' Rights" around their facilities. In Ohio, those rights are the law.

There is an Ohio law that lays out the rights of patients in nursing homes (O.R.C. 3721.13: Residents' Rights). This law is very long and complex, but here are a few examples of parts of this Ohio nursing home law:

- Nursing home residents are entitled to a safe and clean living environment, and to adequate and appropriate medical treatment and nursing care.

- They have the right to be free from physical, verbal, mental, and emotional abuse and to be treated at all times with courtesy, respect, and full recognition of dignity and individuality. Unless they have been adjudicated incompetent, nursing home patients have all of their civil rights.

- Residents have the right to comfort and sanitation, and the right to have all reasonable requests and inquiries responded to promptly.

- They have the right, within certain limits, to a doctor of choice, and the right to withhold payment from any doctor that charged the patient but did not actually visit the patient. The same rights apply to a pharmacist.

- Importantly, the patient has the right to be consulted about and to participate in all care plans that the nursing home will provide for the patient.

- If there is any significant change in the resident's health status, it must be reported to the resident's sponsor. As soon as such a change is known to the home's staff, the home shall make a reasonable effort to notify the sponsor within twelve hours.

- Nursing home patients are entitled to privacy, including privacy during medical examinations, and they may refuse to be the subject of medical experiments.

- Physical or chemical restraints may only be used for short times or in an emergency and any such restraint lasting more than twelve hours has to be ordered by a physician. This is actually a very complicated clause that a lawyer would need to interpret.

- The patient has the right to use alcohol and the right to use tobacco under house rules. The resident also has the right to get up and go to sleep at any time, as long as meals and the other patients are not disturbed.

- Unless there is a documented legal reason not to, each patient has the right to unrestricted and private communication with family, with social workers, and with anybody else. These communications include visits at any hour, mail and telephone privacy, private spousal visits (or a shared room if both are residents), and the right to "knock before entering" if the door is closed.

- Financially, a nursing home patient has the right to be free from financial exploitation, and to have all of the rates and costs of the home explained. The patient has the right to an individual financial life, and to all of his or her financial records that are kept by the nursing home.

- The patient cannot be transferred without the patient's permission, but that is subject to a number of exceptions (again, please talk to a lawyer about this).

- Patients have the right to voice grievances to anyone, including a patient's rights advocate.

Chapter 5
Confirming Suspicions of Abuse or Neglect

Placing a loved one in the professional care of an Ohio nursing home facility should be a comforting feeling. After all, you expect your loved one will be receiving the level of attention, assistance and respect they not only need but deserve.

Unfortunately, there are frequent occasions when a family's trust and confidence in the care of a loved one are violated by a nursing home facility.

Sometimes the deficiencies in professional care are obvious while other times they are difficult to see. You may suspect something is wrong but you can't confirm your suspicions. You need to know what to look for with abuse or neglect. Then, you need to talk about your concerns with someone who can help you and your loved one.

Here are a few examples that may be indicators of abuse or neglect in an Ohio nursing home or care facility:

- Unexplained or unexpected death.
- Administering medications and/or prescription drugs erroneously.
- Bedsores (also known as pressure sores).
- Falls from lack of supervision or safety measures.
- Poor hygiene or foul odors.
- Bruises or cuts.
- Broken or fractured bones.
- Sudden or significant weight loss.
- Skin rashes or skin tears.
- Dehydration.
- Disorientation.
- Anxiety, fear or depression.
- Inability or reluctance to communicate.
- Use of unnecessary physical or chemical restraints.

Chapter 6
Selecting the Right Nursing Home for Alzheimer's Patients

One of the most difficult conversations that a family will ever have is the decision of whether or not to place a loved one with Alzheimer's disease into an Ohio nursing home. It is very important to be completely prepared and informed about every aspect of this decision. The family needs to look at many variables when deciding which Ohio nursing home would be the best.

There are no specific nursing home regulations that single out Alzheimer's patients for special treatment. So it is important for the family to take charge of the search for the appropriate managed care facility. Alzheimer's patients can be very difficult to deal with, and a family should make absolutely sure that the chosen Ohio nursing home can provide the best possible care. There are no hard-and-fast guidelines for this search but there are a number of proactive actions that a family can take.

First, and before any move, a complete physical and mental assessment of your loved one should be completed. A candid discussion of the individual's needs should be done in the presence of the family and caregivers. Try to decide what the person is really capable of, and in what areas the person needs assistance. Honesty is crucial. An open and honest discussion will help with the selection of a facility, but will also help the staff at the facility get a baseline idea of your loved one's needs.

Next, do your research. You can do online research on the facilities that you are considering at this Medicare website: **www.medicare.gov/NHCompare**.

Next, visit several facilities. Before deciding on a facility at least two visits are in order.

The first visit should be a scheduled visit to get a tour from the staff. If the initial visit passes muster, a second unannounced visit should be made.

The second visit will likely be more telling than a carefully coordinated tour. Do not hesitate to talk with the staff during your visits. You can learn a lot about the facility based on the attitude and demeanor of the staff. A disgruntled staff is often an indicator of unhappy residents.

Find out if the facility takes special care for Alzheimer's patients, even though the law does not require it. Check to see if the home does the following:

Place restrictions on in-and-out privileges for residents. This helps decrease the likelihood of escape and wandering.

Require visitors to sign in. Mentally impaired residents are disproportionately physically and sexually abused compared with the general nursing home population.

Does the facility have a tracking system or alarm for residents who have a tendency to wander? Depending on the mobility of the individual, a surveillance bracelet should be used to keep track of the person.

The facility should have clearly marked walkways inside and outside. The walkways should be well lit, have directional signage with diagrams as opposed to written diagrams.

Have a circular design. Alzheimer's patients get particularly frustrated when running into dead-ends and right angles.

The most important consideration is the experience and training of the staff. They must be able to routinely handle the needs of Alzheimer's patients.

Ask the following questions before you decide on a facility:

- Does the facility require / provide any specialized Alzheimer's training for the staff?

- Does the facility do background checks on all employees?

- What is the policy for alerting a family member to an incident?

- What is the policy for physical and / or drug restraints?

- What is the facility's toileting policy?

- Are diapers changed regularly or does the facility only change on a schedule?

- How does the facility ensure that residents eat?

- Do they have staff to monitor what is and is not eaten?

- What is the resident/staff ratio? A general staffing rule is 1:6 for staffing during the day.

Chapter 7
Elder Abuse vs. Nursing Home Abuse

Although it may seem as if nursing home abuse is the same as elder abuse, they are, in fact, very different areas of the law.

A nursing home abuse case is a civil action (lawsuit) against the nursing home and the staff of a care facility. These lawsuits arise when a resident of one of these facilities is injured as a result of the negligence of the institution. These types of lawsuits often result in both a change of behavior in the nursing home facility and a monetary award to the injured party or their estate.

Elder abuse, on the other hand, is a serious crime, in which an older person is abused by a private party—usually a relative, but it can be a care giver too.

Elder abuse in Ohio nursing homes can take a number of different forms. The type of abuse will determine what kind of responsibility the nursing home will have to take for the abuse—criminal, civil, or both.

While elder abuse in Ohio is a crime, it may also come from circumstances where the nursing home may be sued for damages.

And, many times, elder abuse in nursing homes will give rise to both criminal and civil actions against the home.

If a nursing home employee, or the nursing home itself, has committed a crime, the nursing home may be prosecuted in criminal court by a local or state prosecutor.

There is a very good explanation of this process on the web page of the Ohio Attorney general at:

http://www.ohioattorneygeneral.gov/services/seniors/elder-abuse

If a crime has been committed, our elder abuse and nursing home abuse attorneys can advise you on the proper steps to take in contacting the appropriate authorities.

At the same time, many circumstances of criminal elder abuse may also give rise to an action for civil damages against the nursing home. While money will not make the past abuse go away, monetary damages against a nursing home certainly will make that home think twice about repeating that behavior in the future. In other words, you can sue them even if they have been charged with a crime.

Criminal acts that may also give rise to civil litigation include physical abuse, sexual abuse, and verbal abuse of the resident.

Chapter 8
Legal Actions That Can Be Taken Against Nursing Homes

As the population ages, more and more people will live in nursing homes and assisted living facilities. As the number of residents increases, so too does the potential for abuse, neglect, and other derelictions of duty.

If you or someone you know is being mistreated in a nursing home or other type of long term care facility, many legal remedies are available. Some typical causes of action against nursing homes include the following:

Negligence. This includes:

- Negligent personal supervision and care.
- Negligent hiring and retention of employees.
- Negligent maintenance of the premises.
- Negligent selection or maintenance of equipment.

A nursing home can be held liable for negligence if:

- The nursing home breached a duty of care owed to the injured person.
- The person's injury was caused by this breach.
- The nursing home's conduct caused the injury.

Breach of contract. A nursing home usually enters into a contract with a resident, in which it sets out what services it will provide and the cost of those services. If the abuse or neglect is contrary to promises made in the contract regarding resident care, the nursing home can be sued under a breach of contract theory.

Civil rights violations. Victims of abuse and neglect by government-run nursing facilities can bring a cause of action for violations of the victim's civil rights. The violation is based on the fact that nursing homes are required to care for residents in a manner promoting quality of life, provide services and activities to maintain the highest practicable physical, mental and psychosocial well-being of residents, and conduct comprehensive assessments of their functional abilities.

Consumer protection violations. Consumer protection laws may provide a cause of action against nursing homes that financially exploit the elderly.

Licensing agency investigations. An agency investigation may provide immediate help and relief to the victim and prevent further harm by stripping the nursing home of its license to operate.

False Claims Act. False Claims Act lawsuits may be appropriate if nursing homes failed to provide the care for which they are reimbursed by the government.

Criminal culpability. Criminal prosecutions can be brought for murder, manslaughter, sexual assault, rape, assault and battery, theft, forgery, embezzlement, fraud, and other crimes.

Chapter 9
Understaffed Nursing Homes

Understaffing a nursing home puts patients at risk, yet some corporate owners do it knowingly to boost profits. To uncover evidence of this dangerous and often deadly corporate policy, begin your search with the nursing home's records.

If a nursing home or any other business does not have enough employees to do a job, that job cannot be done properly. In the business of health care, the consequence of understaffing can be catastrophic.

Understaffing is often the reason nursing home patients do not receive appropriate care. Despite an employee's best intentions, if he or she does not have time to provide the necessary care, patients may be harmed.

In a nursing home, staff time is directly related to the ability to provide care. Evidence shows that higher staff levels and lower nurse turnover are linked to fewer pressure ulcers, catheterized patients, and urinary tract infections; less antibiotic use; increased probability of discharge; reduced likelihood of death; and improved patient outcomes.

Understaffing is associated with high urinary catheter use, poor skin care, poor feeding, malnutrition, dehydration, and low participation in activities.

Inadequate food intake is a major reason frail elderly people die in nursing homes. Feeding patients who need assistance with eating, encouraging patients to remain as independent as possible in feeding themselves, and supervising patients at mealtime require substantial staff time. Without it, residents can suffer inadequate nutritional intake, leading to malnutrition, dehydration, and starvation.

Similarly, overworked nursing staff may not have time to keep patients from sitting or lying in one place too long. Patients at risk for skin breakdown require frequent and regular turning and repositioning, often at least every two hours. If the nursing home is understaffed, these patients may not receive the preventive services they need, making their condition more likely to decline.

Government regulators have recognized the danger of understaffing in nursing homes. All nursing homes participating in Medicare must meet certain requirements specified in the Federal Nursing Home Reform Act (FNHRA), which is part of the Omnibus Budget Reconciliation Act of 1987 (OBRA). Those regulations require a facility to have "sufficient nursing staff to provide nursing and related services to attain or maintain the highest practicable physical, mental, and psychosocial well-being of each resident."

Nursing homes must have enough staff to provide all necessary care to all patients on a 24-hour basis. Nursing staff includes not only registered nurses (RNs) but also licensed practical nurses (LPNs/LVNs), trained medication assistants (TMAs), and nursing aides (CNAs). State statutes and regulations also may specify nursing home staffing standards.

Investigation and Discovery

In evaluating whether a nursing home employs sufficient staff to provide patient care, you must consider several factors:

Hours. It is important to note the difference between productive and nonproductive nursing hours. Productive hours involve direct patient care, while nonproductive hours involve administrative nursing staff.

Census. The census is the number of patients living in the facility during the relevant time period.

Acuity. The level of medical complexity of each nursing home patient's illness or condition is called acuity.

Resource utilization groups (RUGs). Medicare reimbursement classifications are established according to a schedule of RUGs. Classification is based on a standardized assessment tool - the minimum data set - which evaluates each patient's physical functioning, disease diagnoses, health conditions, and treatments received. After the assessment is completed, a RUGs classification is assigned to the patient.

Facility case mix score. RUGs are used to determine Medicare's prospective payment to nursing homes. Each RUG is assigned a weight. The sum of all patients' RUG weights is the index. By dividing the index by the total census, you can determine the case mix score.

Per patient days (PPD). The PPD is the total nursing hours for all nurses on duty on any given day, divided by the patient census for the same time period. For example, if the facility has 2 nurses, each working 8 hours, in a facility that has 15 patients, the facility has 1.06 nurse staffing hours PPD (2 x 8 = 16, divided by 15 patients).

As a patient's acuity increases, his or her RUG rating and corresponding reimbursement rate increase. The premise is that a patient with a higher RUG rating will need more care or more skilled care. The RUG system provides for higher reimbursements to facilities when caring for increasingly medically complex patients, because such care must be delivered by more care providers or by providers with higher skill levels.

Some nursing homes market for patients with higher acuity levels. By increasing the acuity of the patient population, the facility can increase its gross revenues. But even when a facility's care requirements increase, the number of skilled staff often does not increase. Staffing analysis requires an understanding of patient population acuity as well as the PPD ratio.

Census, acuity, and staffing levels can be established through documents created by the facility. Ask for the following:

Medicare and Medicaid cost reports. Each skilled nursing facility that participates in the Medicare program is required to submit to the Centers for Medicare and Medicaid Services (CMS) a Medicare cost report. This public report details the facility's annual operating expenses and revenues and can be used to establish its annual census. It includes data regarding beds/bed-days available; inpatient days; annual occupancy rate; RUGs and case mix score; and data regarding employees on payroll, wage index information, and cost allocation. You can also obtain the report by requesting it through the appropriate intermediary, which can be identified at the CMS web site.

Facilities that participate in state Medicaid programs are also required to submit Medicaid cost reports, typically to the state's department of health. This report contains information comparable to that in the Medicare cost report, but reports can differ by state. Medicaid cost reports can be obtained through the health department.

You can use cost reports to show PPD trends in a facility by looking at the patient census and funds allocated annually to direct-care nursing staff. Cost reports also provide direct-care staff retention rates and productive and compensated hours.

Roster/Sample Matrix. Skilled nursing facilities use the Roster/Sample Matrix form (CMS-802) to list all current patients and to note pertinent care categories. Based on this information, federal surveyors select the patient sample they use when conducting the facility survey. This information can be used in establishing facility census and acuity when analyzing staffing levels.

Posted nurse staffing information. Under 42 C.F.R. §483.30(e), the facility must post the total actual hours worked by RNs, LPNs/LVNs, and CNAs, as well as the patient census, every day. The data must be posted in a clear and readable format in a prominent place that is readily accessible to patients and visitors. It must be maintained for at least 18 months. On request, the facility must make nurse staffing data available for review at a reasonable cost.

The §483.30(e) posting establishes the staff-to-patient ratio for any given shift, but it does not reveal the number of staff present at any given time within that shift. Patient needs and the consequent demands on staff may vary throughout the day. For example, demands on aides increase during mealtime, when multiple patients need feeding assistance at the same time.

Punch detail reports. These reports can provide staffing levels at any given time during any given shift. Facilities typically use an automated time-clock system to manage staff attendance and payroll. This way, the facility can precisely identify when every employee was working. Also, manipulating the queries for information in the database can create various punch detail reports, such as the number of employees within the facility, of any given job description, at any given time. This not only identifies the raw data of the number of staff working, but it also may identify caregivers, such as aides, whose names typically do not appear in the patient's chart.

Turnover reports. Administrators and human resources departments typically use the punch detail statistical data to evaluate monthly, quarterly, and annual employee turnover rates. Each nursing home also reports its staffing hours to its state survey agency.

Schedules. Staff schedules represent the staffing decisions the facility has made. But the schedule identifies only who was supposed to work on a shift—the punch detail report identifies who actually worked.

Daily aide assignment sheet. At the beginning of each shift, each nursing aide is given a daily assignment sheet. This document details which patients the aide is assigned to care for, the patients' room numbers, and their needs. To understand an aide's workload, you must know the care needs of that aide's patient population as well as the number of patients he or she is assigned to care for.

Floor plan. The nursing home's floor plan can help you understand how the patient population is distributed among various units and throughout the building, the physical distribution of the patients assigned to nursing staff, and the patients' proximity to the nursing desk.

The nursing home must ensure that it provides sufficient nursing staff to meet the health needs of its patient population.

Chapter 10
Misuse and Overuse of Drugs and Medications

Many nursing home patients are treated with psychiatric drugs. These drugs can often be administered without the consent of either the patient or the family.

In fact, at least one set of statistics shows that 25% of nursing home patients are being treated with psychoactive chemicals. Another set puts the percentage of nursing home patients undergoing psychiatric treatment at over 70%. Florida is even worse, according to a recent New York Times article. Within three months of admission, a team of University of South Florida researchers determined, 71% of Medicaid residents in Florida nursing homes were receiving a psychoactive medication even though most were not taking such drugs in the months before they moved in and didn't have psychiatric diagnoses. Fifteen percent of residents were taking four or more such medications. But only 12% were getting nondrug treatments like behavioral therapy.

Statistics seem to show that the use, or misuse, of psychoactive drugs in nursing homes has risen alarmingly in the last ten years or so. California is at least one state that has had a coalition created to combat the misuse of psychiatric drugs among the elderly.

While there are certainly times in which the use of anti-depressants and other drugs are for the benefit of the patients, it is also true that many nursing homes unfortunately use those kinds of drugs, as well as even stronger drugs, to control patients so that they require less care and attention.

The United States Senate is aware of this problem. Senators Chuck Grassley and Herb Kohl, the co-chairs of the U.S. Senate Special Committee on Aging, recently expressed concerns about the role of nursing home pharmacists in the "overutilization" of anti-psychotic drugs. Citing the financial incentives inherent to pharmacists to increase drug use, the Senators sent a letter on August 1, 2011, encouraging the Center for Medicare Services to take action, via Medicare Part D, to subject anti-psychotic prescriptions to increased oversight. By curbing drug overutilization, the federal government would save money on erroneous payments and residents would be spared the increased mortality associated with anti-psychotics.

If you visit a loved one who was cheery one day and virtually immobile the next, you need to check to see what drugs are being given. The pharmaceutical industry and the lower-skilled nursing staff who only want to control patient behavior may be working against you.

Giving drugs without consent, giving the wrong medication, overmedicating, and using psychoactive drugs to control patients are all signs of nursing home abuse.

Chapter 11
Falls in Nursing Homes

One of the greatest dangers that a resident of a nursing home can face is falling. While all falls cannot be prevented, proper assessment of a resident's fall risk is an integral part of a proper Plan of Care.

This assessment needs to be constantly re-evaluated based upon the changing circumstances of the individual resident. While an initial fall assessment may have been proper upon the admission of a resident, the failure to reassess the resident when a change in circumstances has occurred is neglect which can lead to serious injury or even death. Examples of a change in circumstances include: a first fall in the facility; a change in mental status; a change in medications; or continued decline in vision

The National Safety Council estimates that persons over the age of 65 have the highest mortality rate (death rate) from injuries. Among older adults, injuries cause more deaths than either pneumonia or diabetes.

The rates of fall-related deaths among older adults rose significantly over the past decade. 15,800 people age 65 and older died from injuries related to unintentional falls. About 1.8 million people age 65 and older were treated in emergency departments for non-fatal injuries from falls, and more than 433,000 of these patients were hospitalized (CDC 2005).

Unfortunately, our understanding of the true extent of this danger is handicapped as these documented statistics fall short of the actual number since many incidents are unreported by seniors and unrecognized by family members or caregivers.

Alarming Statistics

- Annually, falls are reported by one-third of all people age 65 and older.
- Two-thirds of those who fall will fall again within six months.
- Falls are the leading cause of death from injury among people age 65 or over.
- Approximately 9,500 deaths in older Americans are associated with falls each year.
- The elderly account for 75% of deaths from falls.
- Up to 40% of people who have a stroke have a serious fall within the next year.
- Nearly 85% of deaths from falls are among people age 75 and older.
- Among people ages 65 to 69, one out of every 200 falls result in a hip fracture, and among those age 85 or over, one fall in 10 results in a hip fracture.
- One-fourth of those who fracture a hip die within six months of the injury.

- Approximately 25% of community-dwelling people age 75 or over unnecessarily restrict their activities because of fear of falling.
- After adjusting for age, the fall fatality rate is 49% higher for men than for women.
- Women are 67% more likely than men to have a non-fatal fall injury.
- Rates of fall-related fractures among older adults are more than twice as high for women as for men.
- About 72% of older adults admitted to the hospital for hip fractures were women (CDC 2005).
- 50% of elderly, living in a nursing facility, suffer a fall each year, and approximately 1,800 die.
- In a 100-bed nursing home, there are 100 to 200 reported falls each year. However, this is quite likely to be a significant underestimate. (Rubenstein LZ. Preventing falls in the nursing home. *Journal of the American Medical Association.* 278(7):595, 1997.)
- The fall incidence in nursing home elderly is three times the rate for non-nursing home elderly.

These statistics highlight the danger that falls pose to residents of nursing homes. As stated earlier, all falls cannot be prevented; however safeguards can and should be utilized for those residents who are a fall risk. Such nursing interventions can be: lowering the resident's bed; putting fall mats around the bed to decrease the chance of injury if a fall occurs; utilizing bed and chair alarms to notify the staff that a resident is attempting to get up and walk when they should not be attempting this activity without assistance; setting up a regular toileting program to reduce independent attempts to utilize the bathroom because of the resident's urgency to avoid soiling themselves and staff unavailability to assist them to a bathroom. These are but a few of the possible interventions that can be utilized to reduce the risk to a nursing home resident.

If you have a loved one in a nursing home, check with the nursing staff to make sure an accurate and updated fall assessment has been performed. If a fall risk is present, make sure fall interventions have been put in place to reduce the chance of harm to your family member. If your family member was a fall risk and these steps were not taken or the risks were ignored, your loved one has been neglected. This is a form of nursing home abuse in Ohio.

Nursing homes in Ohio have the absolute duty to keep their residents free from injury. It is alarming how many preventable falls leading to serious injuries take place in Ohio nursing homes each and every year. According to the Centers for Disease Control and Prevention (CDC), an average nursing home with 100 beds reports 100 to 200 falls annually.

Nearly 1,800 senior adults living in nursing homes die each year from fall-related injuries. Those who experience non-fatal falls can suffer debilitating injuries and have difficulty getting around resulting in reduced quality of life. About 10% - 20% of nursing home falls cause serious injuries, while 2% - 6% cause fractures. The fear of falling can cause further loss of function, depression, feelings of helplessness, and social isolation.

Falls can take place in virtually every area of a nursing home. The next time you visit a nursing home ask the staff whether they are taking every precaution to make sure residents are safe from falls. This includes asking about and verifying:

- Proper lighting.
- Eliminating obstacles.
- Regular eye exams.
- Programs to maintain strength and coordination.
- Monitoring after administration of medication to prevent dizziness.
- Supervision for use of canes, walkers, etc.
- Use of bed rails and constraints.

Chapter 12
Broken Bones and Fractures

Statistics show that eleven million elderly people suffer broken bones annually, which is one out of three elderly Americans. As people age, their bones become more frail, and fractures may occur from even the most ordinary and gentle movement. However, it is also unfortunately true that a fractured bone in an Ohio nursing home patient can be caused by the carelessness of a staff member.

If someone suffered a broken bone while living in a nursing home, it may be difficult to determine if the occurrence was natural, or if it was caused by nursing home abuse or negligence. It may take both medical and legal experts to get to the bottom of any particular injury.

But there are some signs that you can look to when trying to figure out what happened.

One general rule of thumb is to take a look at the type of fracture that the patient has suffered. That can at least help determine that direction that the investigation should take. There are three general types of fractures that elderly people can have: stress fractures, spontaneous (compression) fractures, and traumatic fractures.

Stress fractures are actually tiny cracks in bones caused by overuse and repetitive motion. They occur most commonly in the lower legs and feet because these are weight-bearing bones. Stress fractures may be barely noticeable at first, but the swelling and pain will intensify as they worsen. Therefore, it is important to receive proper care and treatment to prevent the stress fracture from becoming more serious.

Stress fractures would not be caused through the fault of the nursing home, but the staff needs to be aware of the signs of stress fractures and be prepared for treatment as soon as possible. Early treatment of stress fractures is important, so the cracks do not worsen. Treatment includes reduced activity until the bone has a chance to heal.

Spontaneous or compression fractures are bone breaks that occur without trauma in what seem like normal bones. The spine and hips (bones that directly support your weight) are the bones most likely to be affected by spontaneous fractures. Older bones are more vulnerable to compression fractures because they lack the internal support structures to withstand impacts and pressure.

The primary cause of these fractures is osteoporosis, or weak bones. A fracture of this sort can be caused simply by walking, so it is important to personalize individual walking plans for elderly residents according to their bone health, which can be determined by BMD (bone mineral density) tests.

These fractures often take place in the hips or spine. Treatment for a compression fracture can include surgery and a lengthy recovery and rehabilitation period.

Traumatic fractures are caused by an injury. This is often a simple fall. Elderly people are susceptible to dangerous falls because of poor balance and coordination, weakness, changes in gait, poor vision, illness and medications that cause sleepiness or dizziness. If the resident lost consciousness, this could be a sign of a more serious condition, such as a heart attack or stroke.

A traumatic bone fracture could also be a sign of nursing home abuse or neglect.

After an accident or fall, nursing home staff members will examine the injured area to look for bone breaks, cuts, bruising, or other signs of injury. The staff should ask questions and investigate how the injury occurred. This investigation into the cause of the fall is very important to protect the resident and prevent future falls.

But you should also be involved in this investigation. If it appears that there are any irregularities in the fall, treatment, or investigation of a fracture, you will want to consult outside experts to see if the nursing home may be at fault, or if the injury was a natural occurrence.

Chapter 13
Malnutrition and Dehydration

Your loved one is under the care of a nursing home, which must provide adequate food and liquids. But that is not always the case.

Between 1999 and 2002, malnutrition and dehydration killed at least 13,890 nursing home patients nationwide and contributed to the deaths of about 68,000 others.

Nursing homes have a responsibility to provide adequate hydration to their residents, and to provide the proper training to their employees to recognize the signs and symptoms of dehydration.

Many times, these incidents take place simply from the fact that the nursing home staff do not even pay the most basic attention to their patients.

Your loved ones may be at risk for dehydration and malnutrition, and may even be experiencing symptoms of these conditions, and you may not even know it.

Residents with Alzheimer's or dementia, incontinent residents, and residents suffering from colds or the flu are at an increased risk for dehydration.

Patients suffering from dementia may not get thirsty, and are usually unaware that they are dehydrated. They cannot help themselves and, too often, the nursing homes simply do not care enough to pay attention.

As a result of nursing home neglect, dehydration and malnutrition are often found together.

Signs of dehydration and malnutrition are:

- **Sudden weight loss.**
- **Confusion and disorientation.**
- **Sores in the mouth and cracks around the lips**
- **Dry skin**
- **Sunken eyes**
- **Dry mucus membranes**
- **Fever and thirst.**

Health problems and injuries which may result from malnutrition or dehydration include:

- **Fall fractures due to weakness or immobility**.
- **Bedsores**.
- **Loss of muscle mass.**
- **Anemia.**
- **Confusion and disorientation.**
- **Urinary tract infections.**

- **Pneumonia.**
- **Anemia.**
- **Death.**

Causes of dehydration in nursing home residents include:

- **Increased fluid losses due to illness (e.g., diarrhea, infections, fever).**
- **Side effects of medications (e.g., diuretics).**
- **Decreased fluid intake.**
- **Decreased ability of the kidney to concentrate urine.**
- **Decreased thirst sensation.**

Nutritional well-being is an important part of the healthy aging process, and the core issue in the health of Ohio nursing home patients. Unfortunately, malnutrition and other dietary problems in Ohio nursing home patients is a painful reality.

According to a recent study by the Commonwealth Fund, 35% - 85% of nursing home patients suffer from undernourishment.

This is an epidemic, with statistics that make America look worse than a third-world country. Malnutrition in nursing home patients can lead to frailty, organ failure, and even death.

The real tragedy is that malnutrition in nursing home patients is completely avoidable. All that is required is an appropriate evaluation, plan, and food and fluid delivery. Tragically, many nursing homes do not follow simple procedures.

Malnutrition or any improper nutrition is a problem in and of itself. It can also lead to other problems, including infections, confusion, and muscle weakness resulting in immobility and falls, pressure ulcers, pneumonia, and decreased immunity to bacteria and viruses.

Malnutrition is costly; it lowers the quality of nursing home residents' lives, and is often avoidable by simple evaluations and basic care.

Any new nursing home patient must be evaluated for dietary and nutritional needs by the physician. Based on the nutritional assessment, the facility must take steps to ensure that the resident maintains good nutritional health and must provide residents with well-balanced, palatable meals. Any deviation from this plan can be considered to be nursing home abuse.

There are many factors, besides lack of attention that can cause nursing home malnutrition - other causes and conditions that may keep your loved one from receiving adequate amounts of the vitamins, minerals, protein, and calories the resident needs can include: illness; adverse drug effects such as nausea, vomiting, diarrhea, cognitive disturbances, or sleepiness; food and drug interactions which decrease the ability of the body to absorb vitamins and minerals; depression; swallowing disorders; mouth problems like tooth loss, ill-fitting dentures, mouth sores, and mouth pain; and tremors, which affect a patient's ability to feed himself or herself.

But there are other, non-medical causes of malnutrition in nursing home patients which are simply the result of the staff not paying the proper attention to the situation. These can include inadequate attention from staff for residents who need assistance eating; staff who are uneducated about malnutrition and proper ways to feed residents who need help; reliance on liquid supplements; and improper delivery of special dietary needs.

When you visit your loved one, you need to be on the lookout for signs of malnutrition. These signs include loose clothing; cracks around the mouth; pale lips and mouth; complaints about dentures that no longer fit; rapid hair loss; wounds taking longer than normal to heal; confusion (not related to Alzheimer's); skin appearing to be breaking down; sunken eyes; and obvious weight loss.

If your loved one suffers from two or more of these symptoms, you may need to take a closer look at his or her nutrition. You will need answers to some, or all, of the following questions:

- Does it take a long time for the patient to eat?

- Can the patient feed him/herself?

- Is the patient rushed through meals?

- Is the patient unable to finish meals?

- If the patient has a special diet, is it being properly administered?

- Does the patient seem to eat more when someone is there to help with the meal?

- Does the patient seem uninterested in food, or recently lost his or her appetite?

- Does the meal schedule fit the likes and dislikes of the patient?

- Does the patient like the food at the facility?

- Can the patient choose from a menu?

- Are snacks readily available?

- Has the patient started taking any new medications?

- Has the family been informed about any new or sudden weight loss?

- Is the patient's weight routinely monitored?

Malnutrition is insidious. It can creep up on a nursing home patient and kill or cripple before anyone knows what is happening.

Chapter 14
Feeding Tubes

Many residents of Ohio nursing homes need feeding tubes on a temporary or permanent basis, for either a partial supplement or as their only source of nutrition.

Unfortunately, there are times that feeding tubes are not properly inserted by a nursing home staff, resulting in injury and even death.

One primary reason for a feeding tube is cancer, especially of the head, neck, stomach, and esophagus. Other conditions like Crohn's Disease, bowel removal, a stroke, or ALS may also mean that the patient must be fed through a tube. In addition, a resident may need a feeding tube if suffering from severe nutritional problems or dehydration, or if diagnosed with aspirational pneumonia.

Use of a feeding tube, and the nutritional formula that is fed to the patient, must come from a doctor. There are several types of feeding tubes:

- G-Tube is surgically placed into the abdominal wall, below the rib cage and goes directly into the stomach. It is a convenient delivery route for long-term feeding and can be easily replaced.

- PEG (percutaneous esophago-gastronomy) is placed directly into the stomach.

- J-Tube (jejunostomy tube) is surgically placed into the upper section of the small intestine (jejunum). This tube bypasses the stomach and feeds directly into the intestinal tract.

- NG-Tube (nasogastric tube) is placed in a nostril, down the pharynx, through the esophagus, and into the stomach. It is usually used for short-term feeding. The placement of the tube must be checked before each feeding.

There are also several methods for formula delivery:

- The bolus/syringe method uses a syringe attached to the feeding tube. The formula is poured into the syringe and flows into the tube.

- The gravity drip method uses a gravity feeding bag. The flow rate (determined by a doctor) can be controlled, and the bags must be changed every 24 hours to prevent bacteria growth.

- The pump feeding method is controlled by a battery or electrical operated device set to control the rate of infusion.

The food that is passed through the tube can either be a commercial product or a personally-designed formula. A doctor will decide the best plan for feeding based on the resident's gastrointestinal function, physical capability, and degree of cooperation. The feeding formula can range from blended food products to commercial formulas.

A number of things can go wrong with the use of feeding tubes, so resident staff members have to be very careful and mindful when working with a patient who is using one. The feeding tube can become loose and aspiration can still occur with a feeding tube in place. The patient's head must always be above the level of the tube. Bacteria can also grow in the tube. If the tube system has an ice pack to keep the food fresh, the ice must be changed regularly.

If the tube is surgically placed, another set of precautions must be enforced, and another collection of problems can arise. If the right procedures are not followed, infections, choking, and other harm can come to the patient. For surgically placed feeding tubes, great care is needed during the first week after surgery to prevent infection, and also to prevent the tube from pulling away from the abdominal wall.

For tubes placed directly into the stomach, the staff has to make sure that the skin surrounding the tube is kept clean and dry. There are also times when the tube has to be kept covered with gauze.

Another potential problem is gastric leakage, which can occur with stomach feeding tubes. This can be a problem because the gastric juices are acidic and can cause skin irritation if they leak out onto the body of the patient.

If you have a loved one in a nursing home who needs to use a feeding tube, remember that the home needs to take many extra precautions.

Chapter 15
Bedsores

Bedsores, pressure sores and decubitus ulcers form when skin and tissue break down from constant pressure and bad circulation. They occur most often in the hip, lower back, and heel areas. At first, the skin becomes red and irritated. Eventually, open sores develop. If untreated, the condition leads to destruction of muscle and even bone.

Federal law requires that nursing homes have bedsore prevention programs. Yet, bedsores are a primary source of injury to elder patients in nursing homes.

If your loved one has bedsores, pressure sores or decubitus ulcers, it could be from the neglect of nursing home personnel.

Bedsores, pressure sores and decubitus ulcers fall into four categories:

- Stage 1 is an area of skin redness that does not diminish once pressure is relieved.

- Stage 2 is a loss of skin layers that looks like an "abrasion, blister, or shallow crater."

- In Stage 3, a full thickness of skin is lost, exposing tissue. This is described as a deep crater.

- In stage 4, a full thickness of skin and tissue is lost, exposing muscle or bone.

Bedridden nursing home residents may develop bedsores if they receive poor nursing care. To prevent bedsores, a nursing home patient must be moved or repositioned every 2 hours to minimize rubbing, pressure, and friction. Lubricants and protective padding may also be helpful.

Incontinent patients are particularly susceptible to bedsores because exposure to moisture from urine increases the risk of skin damage.

Chapter 16
Seven Entrapment Zones of Bedrails

In the days before modern technology, bedrails were used primarily as a means of confining a nursing home resident to bed. Today, modern bedrails perform a variety of functions associated with a nursing home resident getting into and out of bed, as well as continuing to perform their standard function of restraint.

In fact, a bedrail is the most common form of restraint in a nursing home.

Even with new designs, bedrails commonly cause falls and entrapment, which may result in fractures or even death. In order to help identify potential problems with bedrails, the FDA has identified seven "entrapment zones."

Entrapment occurs when a nursing home resident tries to get out of bed, but is trapped from doing so by a bedrail. Injury often occurs after a bedrail entrapment incident.

Nursing home residents leave, or want to leave, bed for a number of reasons, including the need to use the bathroom, general boredom, breathing difficulties, pain of various kinds, hunger or thirst, agitation, delirium, etc.

Nursing home residents with cognitive impairment are the most likely group to be injured in an incident involving bedrails.

The nursing home can easily implement programs designed to alleviate bedrail entrapment. Simple programs such as scheduled toileting, administration of increased pain medication prior to bed, and identification of residents with delirium can be helpful in preventing bedrail injuries.

Chapter 17
Misuse of Restraints

Use of restraints on nursing home residents is sometimes appropriate, but it must be done under a physician's instructions. These instructions should specify what kinds of restraints may be used, how long they may be used, and under what circumstances.

It is never appropriate to use restraints on residents for a worker's convenience or to punish a resident. In fact, Medicare and Medicaid certified nursing homes are expressly forbidden from using restraints for any purpose other than protecting a resident's physical safety.

One of the most common reasons for using restraints is to prevent residents from falling out of their beds. Rails are sometimes used for this reason, but some nursing homes completely immobilize residents by fastening them to the bed with straps or belts. This is clearly inappropriate when bed railings will suffice, and in most cases, even those are uncalled for.

Nursing home staff should exhaust all other possible solutions before resorting to the use of physical restraints. For example, a resident's bed could be lowered or his or her mattress could be placed on the floor to lessen the danger of a fall. Alternately, workers could check on the resident more frequently or a bed alarm can be used to alert staff to a possible fall.

Sometimes restraints are used to protect the safety of residents besides the one being restrained. People with certain mental disorders are prone to hitting or attacking others, so restraints may be justified. Still, other, less extreme measures should be exhausted first. Can the problem be solved by separating certain residents, for example?

There are many long-term health problems associated with inappropriate use of restraints, including bedsores, muscle atrophy, and dehydration. To prevent these, nursing home staff may have to check on restrained residents more often than non-restrained ones. They must also allow them opportunities to exercise every few hours.

Chapter 18
Clostridium Difficile Infection

Clostridium Difficile, commonly known as "C. Diff," is a type of infection that has been gaining a lot of attention in Ohio nursing homes. This infection can cause severe damage to a nursing home patient, and may come about as the result of treating another disease.

C. Diff is a bacterial infection that can cause diarrhea and more serious intestinal conditions, such as colitis. C. Diff bacteria can be found in the feces of an infected person, and then spread to other patients when caregivers come in contact with the feces of an infected patient and fail to wash their hands before treating another patient.

Many elderly in nursing homes and hospitals are at a heightened risk for contracting C. Diff because they may be taking antibiotics for other diseases. These antibiotics can weaken the body's ability to fight off contagion, and the theory now is that C. Diff comes into an elderly person's body and takes advantage of that weakness.

Curing one problem can simply cause another one.

When diagnosed early on, C. Diff may be treated with a course of specialized antibiotics. But, of course, the disease has to be recognized to be treated, and those antibiotics only work properly if the infection is caught and treated early.

Advanced cases of C. Diff may require surgery in the bowel or colon and may be deadly. There are even reported cases of nursing home deaths from C. Diff.

Chapter 19
Physical Therapy Abuse or Neglect

Most people are aware that doctors, nurses, and nursing homes can be sued for medical malpractice. Physical therapists (PTs) fall into this category, too.

Physical therapy is becoming more and more popular as an alternative treatment for nursing home residents. At the same time, the threat of abuse or neglect while a nursing home resident undergoes physical therapy rises as well.

Physical therapy is supposed to help improve a nursing home resident's physical well-being. In skilled nursing facilities, injuries can occur during a physical therapy session for any number of reasons, including the physical therapist's unfamiliarity with the patient, inadequate supervision, broken equipment, etc.

When an injury to a nursing home patient occurs during a physical therapy session, you or your loved one may have a cause of action for medical malpractice or negligence. This will include any injury or death because of the negligent actions of the physical therapist, and includes actions that should not have been taken, as well as actions that should have been taken, but were not.

A physical therapist (PT) owes each patient the duty to fully investigate his or her signs and symptoms in order to diagnose and treat the patient properly. A court of law can hold a physical therapist responsible/liable for an error, omission, or negligent act that results in harm.

Some examples of physical therapist malpractice can include:

- **Dropping patients.**
- **Leaving patients unattended on equipment.**
- **Failure to supervise.**
- **Using broken equipment.**
- **Sexual assault.**
- **Over-extending joints.**
- **Failing to inform patients of risks.**

One recent study on physical therapy malpractice revealed that treatment-related events and events related to improper technique were the most common reasons for a malpractice report.

A successful negligence case against a physical therapist will require you to prove that the injured party: (1) was owed a duty from the physical therapist; (2) the physical therapist breached the standard of care; (3) this breach caused harm to the person; and (4) there was actual harm or "damages" to that person.

If you or a loved one is a nursing home resident receiving physical therapy, it is important to understand the medical necessity of physical therapy and its associated risks. Also, be aware that your physical therapist must be licensed by the state to ensure that the person is qualified to perform physical therapy.

Many states, including Ohio, regulate physical therapists. In Ohio, PT's are regulated and licensed by the Ohio Occupational Therapy, Physical Therapy, and Athletic Trainers Board (found at **http://otptat.ohio.gov**).

According to their website, the board was established in 1976 as the Occupational Therapy Board. In 1977, regulation of physical therapy was transferred from the Medical Board to the Ohio Occupational Therapy and Physical Therapy Board. In 1990, licensure of athletic trainers was added to the responsibility of the Ohio OTPTAT Board.

The regulation of the three professions includes: issuing and renewing the licenses of properly qualified individuals; investigating complaints against licensees; monitoring compliance with mandatory continuing education requirements; and educating licensees and the consumers of the services provided by the Board's licensees on the laws and rules that govern the practice of occupational therapy, physical therapy, and athletic training in Ohio and the Board's role to promote and protect the health of the citizens of Ohio through effective regulation of these three professions.

Physical therapists may also be covered individually by malpractice insurance to shield their personal assets and ensure that there are adequate funds to make amends for wrong-doing. A PLI policy covers errors, omissions, or negligent acts.

For elderly nursing home residents, these injuries can be even more dangerous because of their weak bones and underlying medical conditions.

Chapter 20
Inaccurate and Altered Medical Charts

There are times when a medical worker or other nursing home employee might deliberately hide or change paper or electronic medical records. In the state of Ohio, the law clearly states that proof of tampering with such records can be taken as evidence of malpractice, and additionally, it can support a claim for punitive damages.

It is important that you have a skilled Ohio nursing home abuse lawyer to assist you with your case if you suspect that you or a loved one has had your medical records changed.

Attorneys can utilize the services of forensic computer specialists and experienced medical advisers to look for the various signs of records tampering, such as destroying, deleting, or backdating documents; changing certain values; forging signatures; and many other types of document fraud. Pre-trial discovery rules let attorneys get evidence from computer files and storage drives to tell if records were digitally altered.

Although it can be a tough task to show that there was actual intent to change the documents, the motivation to do so can quite often be inferred based on the circumstances. For example, an Ohio nursing home abuse lawyer can often demonstrate that the nursing home employee was aware of a mistake that led to a resident's injury and he or she attempted to hide it in a paper or digital file.

Furthermore, fraudulent additions that are made to records for the purposes of hiding an incident can be discovered by the use of technology. Expert document examiners, who are given access to the original medical record in order to examine them for tampering, can detect things such as differences in ink and indentations that are caused by writing. The examiners can also conduct a chemical analysis of the document.

Chapter 21
Financial Abuse

Ohio nursing home patients are not only subject to physical abuse. They are also targets of any number of scams aimed to get at their money - both from inside and from outside the managed care facility. Ohio nursing homes and managed care facilities can be in a position to control the entire economic life of a patient. Because of that, it is imperative that a family member monitor every penny that the patient receives and spends from every source.

Scams against nursing home patients, and other ways of separating these helpless people from their money, can come in many forms -from con men of various kinds (consumer fraud), to various people who work at the nursing home, and even from family members. Just recently, several scams against nursing home patients have made headlines around the country, however, many of these crimes are never reported or even discovered.

Those kinds of scams are almost too numerous to list. Here are just a few examples:

- A nursing home reassigned Social Security benefits while the patient was under the influence of psychiatric medication.

- A nursing home worker befriended an elderly patient and stole more than $80,000 from him.

- A social worker stole tens of thousands of dollars from multiple people.

- A nursing home worker took more than $4,000 from a patient just by, apparently, using that patient's ATM card.

Examples of financial exploitation also can include cashing an elderly person's checks without authorization, forging a senior's signature, stealing an older person's money or possessions, or deceiving an older person into signing any contract, will, or other document.

The elderly are particularly susceptible to economic scams, especially if they are beginning to lose control of their mental faculties. Often, the misuse of a patient's money can go hand-in-hand with treatment for the signs of dementia, or even with the misuse of psychiatric medication.

The list of different ways to separate the elderly from their money is virtually endless. This is especially true if the elderly person is in a nursing home because the elderly person is completely dependent on that nursing home for every part of his or her life.

While theft from family members is beyond the scope of what we do as nursing home abuse attorneys, there are still warning signs to look for to help determine whether or not your loved one is being subjected to any kind of financial abuse.

In general, people who are monitoring their loved ones who reside in nursing homes should be on the lookout for:

- Sudden changes in bank account or banking practice, including an unexplained withdrawal of large sums of money by a person accompanying the nursing home resident.

- Inclusion of additional names on a nursing home resident's bank signature card.

- Unauthorized withdrawal of the nursing home resident's funds using the resident's ATM card, or any other unauthorized activity in a bank account, credit card account, or investment account.

- Abrupt changes in a will or other financial documents.

- Unexplained disappearance of funds or valuable possessions.

- Substandard care being provided or bills unpaid despite the availability of adequate financial resources.

- Discovery of a nursing home resident's signature being forged for financial transactions or for the titles of his/her possessions.

- Sudden appearance of previously uninvolved relatives claiming their rights to a nursing home resident's affairs and possessions.

- Provision of unnecessary services.

- Secretive loans taken by family members from the elderly person.

- Frequent/recent property title changes or will changes.

- Forced to sign over control of finances unwillingly.

- No/limited money for food, clothes, and other amenities.

If a loved one thinks that he or she is being exploited financially, please listen to that person and ask for detailed financial information from the nursing home or managed care facility.

Chapter 22
Wandering Away from a Nursing Home

One would think that the most basic part of caring for nursing home patients is making sure that they are in the nursing home. Shockingly, nursing home patients wander away from their facilities and are injured or even killed. Many of those injuries happen on or very near to the nursing home's grounds.

Technically, wandering (also referred to as elopement) refers to a cognitively impaired person moving about a nursing home or long-term care facility without appreciation for where they are going. In some cases of patients suffering from Alzheimer's or dementia, the patient may attempt to leave the facility.

A nursing home resident's propensity to wander / elope should be identified in an initial care plan and preventative measures should be implemented by the facility. In a study involving over 15,000 cognitively impaired nursing home patients, researchers from the International Research Consortium on Wandering found that one in five were prone to aimless wandering through nursing home facilities, putting themselves at increased health risk. This study indicates that these are serious problems throughout nursing homes in the United States.

Some of the stories of nursing home patients wandering from their facilities are tragic, and have led to injury and even death. If a nursing home's negligence in allowing a patient to wander causes an injury to that patient, or even a fatality, that nursing home may be facing legal consequences.

Although fairly rare, it is enough of a problem that wandering was directly addressed in the federal Nursing Home Reform Act of 1987. That law requires nursing homes to provide residents with adequate supervision to prevent wandering or elopement. A nursing home may be found liable for failing to prevent wandering or elopement while a patient is in its care.

Injuries associated with wandering can include an increased incidence of weight loss, fatigue, sleep disturbance, getting lost, injuries as a result of falling and untimely death. Nursing home residents who elope may get lost, may not be able to find the way back to the nursing home, and may suffer from heat or cold exposure or another medical crisis.

One recent case even found a wandering patient drowned in a puddle in front of the nursing home itself. Another case involved a nursing home which had an "open door" policy of allowing residents to come and go as they pleased. This resident, who was under medication and had Alzheimer's disease, died in a field down the street from the facility

Close supervision of residents suffering from dementia or Alzheimer's disease is necessary in order to prevent wandering and elopement. Several factors can increase the likelihood of a nursing home resident becoming injured as a result of wandering or elopement. These include:

- **Failure to hire adequate staff to properly supervise the resident.**
- **Failure to properly train staff on how to supervise residents.**
- **Failure to install alarms or other safety devices to prevent wandering.**

These kinds of tragedies can easily be prevented. Common preventative measures should include:

- **Providing an adequate number of staff to supervise residents.**
- **Training nursing home staff on how to identify wanderers.**
- **Using bed, wheelchair or door alarms.**
- **Re-directing patients who are wandering.**
- **Utilizing door and window alarms.**

Nursing homes must acknowledge the risks associated with patient wandering and elopement and take steps to minimize incidents from occurring in the first place. When facilities fail to implement preventative measures, they may be held responsible for the resulting patient injuries.

Chapter 23
Food Quality

Food complaints are among the most common complaints in Ohio nursing homes. Patients look to food for comfort throughout the day, and can easily be made to feel distressed if the food situation is not right. Ohio nursing home patients rely on their care providers to give them the best possible food. But there are many times when that is not the case.

Malnutrition is only one potential problem with the delivery of food to nursing home patients. There are actually positive tasks that every managed care facility in Ohio needs to engage to properly care for their patients. Anything short of this may constitute abuse, or may be a clue that there is an abusive situation going on.

Among the responsibilities for food delivery to their patients, Ohio nursing home facilities are responsible for these factors:

- All meals must meet recommended dietary allowances for each person, based upon age and sex;

- At least three meals should be served daily, at a regular time, with not more than a 14-hour span between a substantial evening meal and breakfast;

- Menus for the current week should be posted in the dining room or other public place;

- Hot foods should be served hot and cold foods should be served cold;

- Meals should be served in an appetizing and sanitary fashion;

- Supplemental fluids and special nourishments should be provided if ordered by the physician;

- The facility must provide each resident with sufficient fluid intake to maintain proper hydration and health;

- Based upon a resident's comprehensive assessment, the facility needs to ensure that a resident (1) maintains acceptable, measurable signs of nutritional status, such as body weight and protein levels, unless the resident's clinical condition demonstrates that this is not possible; and (2) receives a therapeutic diet where there is a nutritional problem;

- Nutritious snacks should be offered several times daily;

- Food should be served cut, ground, chopped, pureed, or in another manner which meets a patient's specific needs;

- Medicare and Medicaid certified nursing homes must consider your personal preferences. If the patient refuses the food, he or she should be offered a substitute with similar nutritional value.

The nursing home facility's physician is responsible for identifying any special dietary needs that a patient may have. The nursing home must have a dietary or food services supervisor in charge of meal preparation who meets state training requirements. The food services supervisor should be a trained dietician.

If a nursing home patient needs a special diet that has to be provided. The doctor will need to prescribe a special diet and give it to the food services supervisor. The food services supervisor may also be able to assist with arranging a special diet directly.

Nursing homes are required to assist patients who need help being fed. This assistance should be provided at the time meals are served so that hot food is still hot and cold food is still cold. The nursing home should ensure that you eat a sufficient amount of food to meet your nutritional needs. If you can feed yourself but need supervision, adequate supervision should be provided regardless of whether you eat in the dining room or your own room.

Good amounts of nutritional and fluid intake are very important to the elderly and those with illnesses. If a nursing home patient has complaints about food, meal service or special dietary concerns, bring them to the attention of the food services supervisor. If this does not bring the necessary changes, take your complaints to the administrator of the home.

Chapter 24
Injuries While Being Moved Within a Nursing Home

As people age, many begin to experience difficulty walking. This can lead to an inability to care for one's self by cooking, bathing, and cleaning which causes some people to enter nursing homes.

Many nursing residents can walk with the help of a mobility aid like a cane or a walker. But even those who can walk unassisted may have difficulty sitting up from a reclining position or standing after they've been sitting.

Nursing home transport injuries occur when an employee causes a resident to fall or handles him or her too roughly while helping the resident change positions or transfer into or out of a wheelchair. Though these injuries can seem like accidents, they could actually be the result of penny-pinching by nursing home administrators or poor training of employees.

How Transport Injuries Happen

Falls are the most common type of injury for senior citizens, and bathing or showering are particularly dangerous. Consider all the steps involved in giving a person a bath if he or she has mobility problems.

First, a nursing home worker needs to move the resident into a wheelchair or help him/her walk to the bathroom. Then the worker needs to undress the resident and help him/her get into the bathtub. After bathing the resident, the worker needs to dry and dress him/her and take him/her back to their room.

This can be exhausting for the resident and the worker, and if the worker isn't physically strong enough to lift the resident, an injury can occur. Handling senior citizens requires not just strength but a gentle touch because their bones tend to be brittle. You can't lift an elderly person the same way you would a bag of groceries.

There are safety devices that help seniors transfer into and out of bathtubs, but some nursing home administrators try to save money by not purchasing this equipment. Workers are also frequently under trained as a cost-cutting measure, so they may not know how to use the equipment they do have.

Chapter 25
Injuries While Being Transported Outside a Nursing Home

Perhaps the most common complaint by nursing home residents is that they feel they have lost their freedom. To combat this, some nursing homes plan day trips to places like museums or shopping malls. Although this gesture is appreciated by most residents, it presents some unique opportunities for injury.

One risk is that the person transporting the residents could get in a traffic accident. Because most nursing homes use large vans or buses for these occasions, the risk of an accident may actually be somewhat higher than normal. These large vehicles handle differently and have more blind spots than smaller cars. The average person has not driven this type of vehicle before. Nevertheless, these vehicles are sometimes entrusted to inexperienced workers.

Of course, any road trip poses some risk of traffic accidents, so this is not unique to nursing homes.

However, the problems that arise when transferring elderly residents in and out of vehicles are unique. If residents are in wheelchairs or have trouble stepping up into a vehicle, the nursing home may have installed some sort of lift to help them.

These lifts, like any machinery, are at risk for breaking or malfunctioning, and this risk increases as they age (especially if they are not properly maintained). Sometimes minor problems are ignored because it is deemed too expensive to address them. For example, a wheelchair lift may start making strange sounds or shuddering when it used to run quietly and smoothly.

Nursing homes owe a standard of care to their residents, and they must prevent any foreseeable injuries. Being aware that a piece of equipment is dangerous but failing to fix it is not just unsafe. It is also a violation of the nursing home's duty to its residents.

It is unfortunate that some nursing homes try to increase their profitability by cutting corners when it comes to maintenance.

Chapter 26
Necessity of an Autopsy in a Nursing Home Abuse Death Claim

We are often asked whether it is absolutely necessary to have an autopsy performed in order to pursue an investigation into a wrongful death claim arising from a suspicious death in a nursing home. The simple answer to this question is no, it not absolutely necessary, but it can be of significant help in determining whether abuse or neglect caused the death of a loved one.

Often the doctor who lists the cause of death of a nursing home resident will list a chronic condition, such as congestive heart failure unless there has been something extraordinary that he becomes aware of prior to issuing a death certificate. This path of least resistance makes it much more difficult to prove that the death was in fact caused by a lack of proper medical care. Without an autopsy to prove otherwise, this type of case produces a long uphill battle for the family of the loved one who has died. Studies reveal that nearly half of the listed causes of death on death certificates for older persons with chronic or multi-system disease are inaccurate. (Miles SH. Concealing accidental nursing home deaths. HEC Forum. 2002 Sep;14(3):224-34). The autopsy rate of nursing home residents is only 0.8 percent.(Katz PR, Seidel G. Nursing home autopsies. Survey of physician attitudes and practice patterns. Arch Pathol Lab Med. 1990 Feb;114(2):145-7). In reality, if an autopsy is not requested, the actual cause of death may never be known.

If there is any indication that a nursing home resident may have died as the result of neglect or abuse, an autopsy should be requested. If the doctor or nurse says there is no need to notify the medical examiner, or if the medical examiner declines to do an autopsy, the next of kin should still consider having an autopsy done. Autopsies help answer questions about what really happened.

As was said not by lawyers, but by practitioners in the field of medicine, "The autopsy is the ultimate 'peer review.' Yet the autopsy has nearly disappeared from hospitals in the United States and around the world." Understandable concern about lawsuits is a huge deterrent to autopsy in spite of the obvious potential for educational, clinical, and research gains. (Geriatrics. 2008 December; 63(12): 14–18, The autopsy and the elderly patient in the hospital and the nursing home: Enhancing the quality of life, Leslie S. Libow, MD and Richard R. Neufeld, MD).

Simply put, if you have any question regarding the cause of your loved-one's death while they were a resident in a nursing home, you should request an autopsy. Knowing the answer to that question will provide not only help if you are considering a cause of action against the nursing home, it will also provide peace of mind.

Chapter 27
Examples of Nursing Home Abuse

Case 1: Wrongful Death

The death of a 78-year-old nursing home resident led to the filing of a wrongful death lawsuit. The suit claims that nurses failed to seek medical attention for the woman after she fell.

The deceased was considered a high fall risk, which required staff to take proactive measures to guard the woman's safety. According to the lawsuit, a care plan was in place but wasn't followed. By this plan the woman's bed should have been kept in a low position, and floor mats should have been in place to soften a fall. Neither of these measures was taken, nor was a bed alarm used.

The lawsuit also contends that nurses were not adequately trained to deal with the woman's injuries. She suffered neurological injuries and bleeding. Rather than call emergency personnel, nurses merely placed the woman back in her bed. She was later found unresponsive, and was then taken to the hospital, where she died.

Wrongful death charges also contend that the nursing facility has refused to release medical records to the deceased family's attorneys, and has failed to produce the name of their own lawyers or contact information. The family earlier attempted to settle out of court for $275,000.

Case 2: Nursing Home Fined for Abuse and Neglect

A nursing home facility was fined over $20,000 for subjecting residents to neglect, mistreatment, and possible abuse. The Federal Centers for Medicare and Medicaid Services imposed the fine after a survey of the facility exposed incidents out of keeping with acceptable practices.

The allegations stem from two incidents. In one, a licensed practical nurse failed to provide care to a tracheostomy patient. She refused to suction the man, and would not allow him to call his mother. Suctioning is a normal and expected procedure for these patients, and is performed to help the patient breathe. In the end the patient was able to contact a friend through Facebook, indicating that he did not feel safe in the care of the nurse in question. While the supervising nurse ultimately did suction the patient, she did not reprimand the nurse in question.

The patient made an additional complaint later that a nurse practitioner removed his Passy-Muir valve. This made it impossible for him to speak.

Inspectors for the survey also cited staff for failing to investigate injuries to the face of another patient.

The facility administrator submitted a plan of corrective action in the case. In the report, he indicates that the one nurse was fired for "reasonable cause that abuse may have occurred." He claimed in the same report that his staff took immediate measures.

Case 3: Nursing Home Indicted for Abuse of Mentally Ill Patient

A nursing home facility was indicted at a grand jury hearing for felony abuse and neglect of a mentally ill patient. The victim died as the result of alleged lack of staff training and care.

The nursing home facility faces charges for the death of a patient with a history of mental illness. The individual made repeated attempts to commit suicide during his stay at the facility. On one occasion he set off a fire extinguisher in his mouth. Another time he wheeled himself out of the facility and into the street in order to be hit by a car.

After each suicide attempt the mentally ill man was hospitalized, then later returned to the facility. He finally succeeded in his suicide attempts by again using a fire extinguisher inside his mouth. What the nursing home staff did to try to prevent him from his attempts is not clear, but the charges indicate the facility did not train employees on how to properly care for mentally ill residents.

Case 4: Nursing Home Employees Charged

A nursing home came under investigation for continued abuse of one of its residents by eleven different caregivers in what may be one of the largest nursing home abuse cases in history.

The victim is a gentleman who resided at the facility for seven years. He was subjected to neglect, assault, and forgery by employees at the nursing home which has been in operation since 1978. The victim's wife has filed a $10 million lawsuit against the center and 35 of its employees.

The wife of the nursing home patient described visiting her husband, returning 12 hours later, and finding his diaper had not been changed. He was rarely shaved, was kept filthy, and his dentures were never removed and cleaned. When food would be brought to him, none of the caregivers would assist him, in spite of the fact that he was known to be unable to feed himself. Roaches were also found on his food tray.

When asked if she would mind FBI agents videotaping her husband's room, she jumped at the chance. The resulting footage was shocking. On one occasion, a registered nurse held a pillow over the victim's mouth and face. Video also showed a nurse's aide throwing popcorn at the victim, laughing all the while as the elderly man fearfully tried to bat it away.

Two employees have already been convicted, and another eleven await trial.

Case 5: Alzheimer's Patient Abuse by Nursing Home Staff

An elderly Alzheimer's patient in a Cleveland, Ohio facility was abused by a nursing home assistant. The worker has pleaded guilty to misdemeanor charges.

The son of the resident had become suspicious of neglect and abuse and placed a miniature hidden video recorder in the air purifier of his mother's bedroom.

Videotape revealed repeated acts of abuse and neglect. The defendant pleaded guilty to misdemeanor assault in an apparent plea bargain by which she will serve not more than six months in county jail. A second defendant in the case pleaded guilty to numerous counts of felony neglect and abuse.

The son of the victim has revealed that two other individuals whom he saw in the video abusing his mother were released without charges. These individuals were terminated by the company. The nursing home fired the two but has not made any comments regarding this facet of the case. The son claims that these workers were not charged because of the way Ohio law is defined in such cases. He also suggested that the convicted had abused his mother more than once, but was only given one count.

Case 6: Physical Abuse and Theft in Nursing Home

A nursing home has been charged with abusing and stealing from elderly residents. The facility has been closed by the state and its license suspended.

Investigation have been conducted at the facility numerous times over the past several years, and in many instances, fines issued for non-compliance with state regulations. The most recent investigation revealed that workers at the nursing home stole Social Security checks from residents and deposited them in their own accounts. In addition, caregivers took money from elderly residents for purchases and failed to return what was left over.

The investigation also found that at least one resident was physically abused. When an elderly woman became angry with staff and started shouting, she was grabbed by the ankles and dragged down the hall as she screamed and kicked. In that instance police were called to investigate, and the woman was subsequently removed to another facility.

Among the arguments cited for closing the nursing home and revoking its license was that, given a history of offenses by the staff, residents were not safe.

Case 7: Verbal Abuse from Nursing Home Staff

While it may seem a relatively minor annoyance for an elderly resident to endure verbal abuse from nursing home staff, one should consider the circumstances. Residents are generally not able to simply leave a facility, due to physical limitations. Moreover, they often live with continual discomfort and likely miss their homes.

From this perspective, one may gain a greater appreciation for difficulties residents endured at a facility in which reports of verbal abuse have become public. The facility was investigated over allegations that nursing staff were rude and verbally abusive to residents.

An administrative officer with the governing corporation stated that their philosophy is to keep the residents first in their minds. He went on to say that in this instance a few employees failed to abide by the company standards. He further indicated that these individuals were no longer with the company.

Along with the employees who committed the acts of verbal abuse, the facility failed because the acts were not immediately reported nor dealt with. The facility then failed overall to provide an appropriate and respectful living environment for its residents.

The administrative officer suggested that the company is regarding this as a learning experience for nursing staff. The lesson apparently is that they are to remember the residents' best interests come first.

Chapter 28
Why You Should Talk to a Nursing Home Abuse Attorney and How an Attorney Can Help with No Out of Pocket Costs to You

Nursing home abuse cases in Ohio can get very complicated. Many of these cases require expert opinions and testimony from medical professionals to decisively prove nursing home abuse has occurred.

A free consultation with an experienced nursing home abuse lawyer can answer many questions you may have. An attorney can also provide guidance on the best course of action to get the help and assistance you need to stop the abuse and prevent it from happening to someone else.

What an Experienced Nursing Home Abuse Lawyer Will Do For You

Every lawyer is different but here is just a sample of what we do at our law firm for our nursing home abuse clients:

- Conduct a free initial consultation and answer all questions.

- Explain the nursing home abuse claim process in detail.

- Explain Ohio laws relating to nursing home abuse.

- Explain the litigation process.

- Prepare and file all necessary and required documents for the nursing home abuse claim and lawsuit.

- Perform an investigation of the claim, including interviewing witnesses, assembling all incident reports, medical reports and other necessary evidence and records to support the claim.

- Engage professional experts to assist in investigations, evaluations and the preparation of reports, including physicians specializing in nursing home care.

- Analyze all laws and cases pertinent to a client's nursing home abuse claim.

- Conduct negotiations with the owners of a nursing home to attempt to obtain a fair and reasonable settlement prior to a trial.

- Prepare all requests for the production of information from the defendant.

- Conduct all necessary depositions.

- Prepare the client for depositions.

- Thoroughly prepare for trial.

- Prepare and file briefs and motions as necessary.

- Represent the client at all hearings and trials.

- Answer all client questions and communicate with the client at all times.

As you can see, the time and effort to handle a nursing home abuse claim is extensive. If you are not familiar with Ohio law, trial procedures, legal document preparation, interacting with other lawyers and negotiating with large companies, your nursing home abuse case can quickly become overwhelming and highly stressful.

Contingency Fee Agreement: The Best of Both Worlds

Understandably, many people are reluctant to speak with or hire an attorney because of the perceived cost. They simply cannot afford to write checks for thousands of dollars each month waiting for a settlement or a verdict in their case.

Fortunately, there is an arrangement where you can utilize the experience and knowledge of an experienced nursing home abuse attorney without needing to pay monthly legal fees while your claim is being pursued.

Our law firm, like many others, represents clients on what is known as a contingency fee basis. With a contingency fee agreement, a lawyer will defer his or her fee until the case is successfully resolved and finalized.

The fee is based on a percentage of the settlement or verdict obtained in the case. If no settlement is received or nor amount is awarded in a verdict, there will be no fee to the attorney.

Contingency fees allow people to hire the best legal representation possible without the risk of losing thousands and thousands of dollars.

The costs associated with a claim are different than the contingency fee. Costs associated with a claim include, but are not limited to, such things as expenses incurred while investigating a claim and prosecuting in the court system. Examples of these costs may include court costs, deposition fees, expert witness fees and record retrieval expenses. In the state of Ohio, a lawyer is allowed to advance these costs on behalf of the client and then recover the costs by deducting them from the compensation a client receives at the conclusion of the case.

There is no reason for you not to at least speak with an experienced nursing home abuse lawyer if you or a loved one has become a victim.

A fear of the unknown prevents a lot of people from moving forward and getting themselves out of problematic situations. We sincerely hope this book has given you a basic understanding of nursing home abuse and a general direction of how to proceed in an effort to stop nursing home abuse in Ohio.

If you would like to talk to us about your nursing home abuse case, we invite and welcome your call. We can be reached at 1-800-297-9191 for your free consultation.

The Authors

The Ohio law firm of Slater & Zurz LLP is a team of legal professionals dedicated to helping others who have become victims of all types of accidents, injuries and nursing home abuse. The law firm has been entrusted to handle more than 30,000 personal injury type cases and has helped clients receive in excess of $150 million in settlements and verdicts.

The lawyers at our law firm have handled over 600 nursing home abuse cases throughout all areas of Ohio.

Attorney Jim Slater is the managing partner of Slater & Zurz LLP and has been actively practicing law for over 40 years. When Mr. Slater is asked what the law firm of Slater & Zurz LLP does, he replies simply by saying,

"We Make Others Do What They Do Not Want To Do."

"We make the decision makers at insurance companies pay fair and proper compensation to victims of accidents.

We make wayward partners pay those they treated unfairly.

We make individuals and businesses pay their customers and employees the money they owe them.

We provide comfort to families by financially punishing owners of nursing homes that harm their loved ones.

We convince juries to award our clients the money they deserve.

In all cases, we work tirelessly to be sure our clients get what they are entitled to receive.

Prior to asking for our help, our clients were either denied proper compensation or were uncertain whether they could receive the compensation they deserved.

We have made companies pay millions when they negligently manufactured products that caused serious injuries.

We have made insurance companies pay hundreds of thousands of dollars when the dogs of homeowners they insured attacked innocent children and caused serious injury.

We have made a hospital pay millions when one of their doctors whom they employed caused a child s death.

We made a large company pay millions to its employees when they failed to pay commission income they earned.

At Slater & Zurz LLP, all cases do not involve millions or hundreds of thousands of dollars. Many of our cases involve smaller amounts of money. But there is a common theme. We make companies and people who have or would treat our clients unfairly do what they do not want to do.

This is what we do at Slater & Zurz LLP. This is what we have done for over 30,000 clients over 40 plus years. I am personally proud of the difference we make for our clients. It has been our goal, from the beginning, to make people proud that we are their attorney and pleased with the results we obtain for them. This is what they tell us on a daily basis."

James W. Slater

Free Consultations Are Always Offered at
Slater & Zurz LLP
Akron • Canton • Cleveland • Columbus

Please call toll free
1-800-297-9191

slaterzurz.com
stopohionursinghomeabuse.com

More Useful and Informative Books by Slater & Zurz LLP

When A Dog Bites Fight Back

If you or someone you know becomes the victim of a dog attack in Ohio, you have specific legal rights to take action. This book will help you understand your rights, how to file a dog bite claim and where you can turn for help to make sure you receive a fair amount for the injuries and damages you suffered.

To request your copy, please call 1-800-297-9191 or visit our website focused on the needs of dog bite victims at dogbitesohio.com.

A Wrongful Death in Ohio

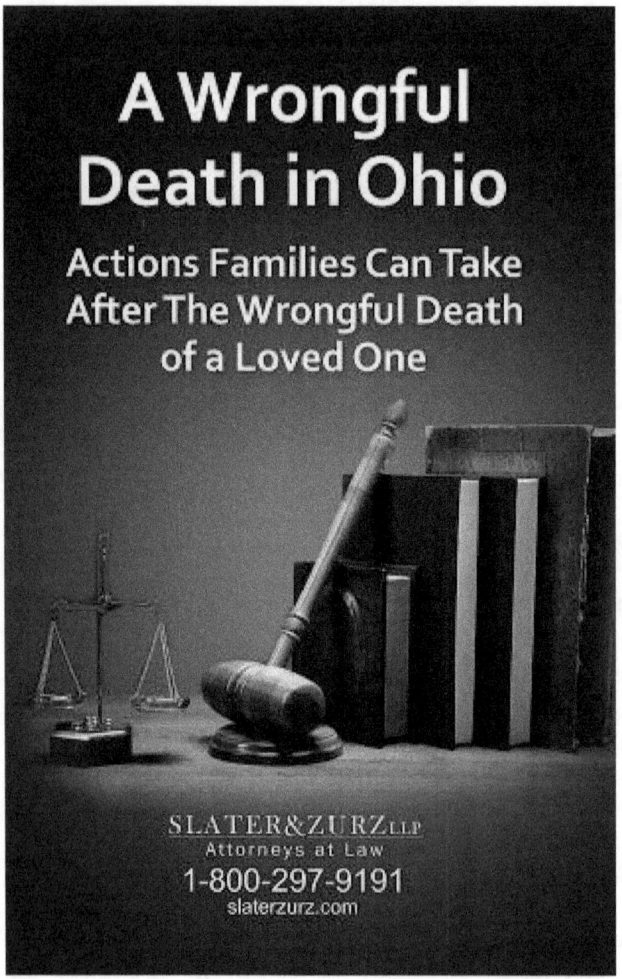

To request your copy please call 1-800-297-9191 or visit our website focused wrongful deaths in Ohio: ohiowrongfuldeathlaw.com

Legal Malpractice in Ohio
How to determine if your lawyer committed malpractice and what to do about it

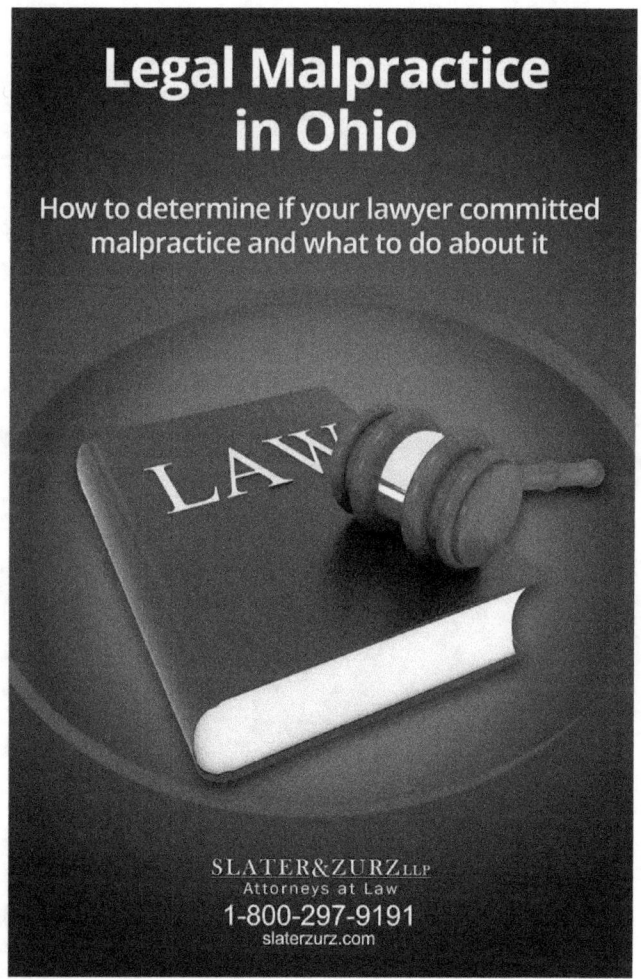

To request your copy please call 1-800-297-9191 or visit slaterzurz.com

www.ingramcontent.com/pod-product-compliance
Lightning Source LLC
Chambersburg PA
CBHW051719170526
45167CB00002B/723